IT OPERATIONS MANAGEMENT
tweet Book01

Managing Your IT Infrastructure in the Age of Complexity

By Peter Spielvogel, Jon Haworth, Sonja Hickey

THiNKaha

E-mail: info@thinkaha.com
20660 Stevens Creek Blvd., Suite 210,
Cupertino, CA 95014

Published by THiNKaha®, a Happy About® imprint
20660 Stevens Creek Blvd., Suite 210, Cupertino, CA 95014
http://thinkaha.com

First Printing: April 2011
Paperback ISBN: 978-1-61699-052-7 (1-61699-052-X)
eBook ISBN: 978-1-61699-053-4 (1-61699-053-8)
Place of Publication: Silicon Valley, California, USA
Paperback Library of Congress Number: 2011926213

The authors are donating all their royalties to the HP Foundation, which funds global disaster relief efforts. The publisher is matching their contribution dollar for dollar.

Advance Praise

"A fast, insightful read for the IT professional, presented in a unique format. A great distillation of IT best practices that will help focus IT goals and facilitate decision making. It's also especially useful for the non-IT manager who needs IT support and wants to understand and influence the decision making process."

Thomas Cheng, President, pcAge, Inc.

"As organizations start to make the transition from traditional IT to the cloud, they will need to adapt their people, processes, and tools. And they will need some guidance that points them in the right direction. This book provides a concise roadmap that will help them along that journey."

Kalyan Ramanathan, VP Marketing, Electric Cloud

"No single IT organization has all the answers to 'IT Operational Management' because sometimes you don't know what questions to ask. This book allows you to start discussions to find the answers you are looking for. It is a great starting point for groups dedicated to process improvement and knowledge sharing."

Henry Wojcik, Manager Operational Monitoring, CME Group

"It's all good common sense that we know we should be doing but don't get the time to do—this little book is a great reference and reminder."

Mark Laird, Technical Consultant, Steria UK Ltd.

"Brilliant format! You'll read it more than once. A thought-provoking source of meaningful discussion topics. You should pass the book around your group to generate ideas and proactive collaboration. The resulting communication is the true value of the text."

Mark Laughlin, Former CIO, The Guitar Center

"*#IT Operations Management tweet Book01* offers a fast-paced, easy-to-read-and-skim resource for meaningfully getting started in planning, preparing, and executing on an IT Operations Bridge. It balances a look at people, process, and technology issues and is careful not to promote one-sided advice that can be applicable in some environments, but destructive in others."

Dennis Drogseth, Vice President, Enterprise Management Associates, Inc.

"The key to successful delivery of Hybrid IT will be collaboration and agreement across organizations, groups, process, and technology, and as such, this view of gaining a common set of principles that can be used for agreement and collaborations, even if they are adjusted specific to the needs of that organization, will be invaluable."

Mark Potts, HP Fellow & VP of Portfolio Strategy , HP Software

---

"In order to meet our customer SLAs, we use a monitoring plan that includes infrastructure, application landscape, incident management, and performance benchmarking. This book distills IT Operations Management to the core elements."

Maryann Phillip, Director of Performance Management, Independence Blue Cross

---

"IT infrastructure management has never been so critical. All business verticals and IT organizations of all sizes will benefit from implementing the ideologies and processes discussed throughout this book—simple IT management techniques which are both enlightening and thought provoking for IT professionals at every level."

Luigi Tiano, Enterprise Management Director, CT Consultants

"The book summarizes years of operations management experience into easy to digest concepts."

Henry Yam, VP of Enterprise Management, Neuberger Berman

Dedication

To my family for their unconditional love and support.
To my parents for their motivation to always pursue excellence.
Peter

To my late mother, who raised three sons single-handedly and did a fine
job. And to my family who tolerate, encourage, and inspire me.
Jon

To my husband, Dan, and my children, Colin, Brianna, and Emma, who
supported me throughout this project. And to my colleagues, Peter and Jon,
who inspired and encouraged me to participate in the writing of this book.
Sonja

Acknowledgments

Thanks to the HP Operations Center products and R&D teams for their tireless efforts.

Thanks to our colleagues, who constantly challenge us to embrace new ideas.

Thanks to our management, who enthusiastically supported this project.

Thanks to our customers, who use their creativity to push the limits of IT management.

Thanks to "eagle eye" Stephanie for her proofreading skills.

Special thanks to Mitchell Levy and the Happy About team for publishing this book.

Peter, Jon, Sonja

Why Did We Write This Book?

Managing IT infrastructure has always been challenging. Virtualization and cloud computing make this task even more difficult. In our daily work, we encounter organizations struggling with these issues.

IT professionals want simple actionable ideas that will deliver gains in availability, performance, and efficiency. We wrote this book with that in mind. Good IT is good business.

Peter Spielvogel, Jon Haworth, Sonja Hickey

Blog: www.hp.com/go/ITOpsBlog
Twitter: *@HPITOps*
Email: ITOpsBook@gmail.com

Managing Your IT Infrastructure in the Age of Complexity

Contents

Preface

Our goal is not to make you an expert on managing IT infrastructure, but to make you and your peers think in a different way about some of your decisions. If our guidance starts a discussion in your team that results in you avoiding one big mistake, then we have achieved our goal.

Section I
IT and the Business

At the start of the dot-com era, people predicted that someday all businesses would become "e-businesses." That time is now. Strong alignment between business and IT is more important than ever. The key to success is communication of shared goals in a common language.

1

IT Operations tools are a business solution. They are not "toys for IT." Justify investment based on business benefits, not benefits for IT.

2

Using an IT monitoring solution proactively can create a competitive advantage in the marketplace by improving quality of service.

3

Manage risk proactively. A major IT outage can hurt your company reputation, bottom line, and even the stock price.

4

Application owners ask 3 questions: Is my app available? Does my app perform well? Is my app secure? You must provide the answers with data.

5

Prioritize IT response to incidents based on business impact. Your business users can tell you which processes are most important.

6

Different roles use different metrics: CIO—service level, cost of IT per app; NOC manager—availability, MTTR; app owner—revenue, risk.

7

Be transparent—show service-level metrics to business owners to instill confidence.

8

Your line of business owners care deeply about risk. They will fund investments in new tools if they can reduce downtime risk.

9

Cost/Minute of Downtime

* Average Outage Time

* Outages/Year

= Cost justification

for investing in a better

monitoring solution.

10

Align monitoring with business criticality. Invest in top-tier functionality when needed; otherwise, optimize spending.

11

Measure the return on investment for any new IT Operations tools or initiatives you implement.

12

Monitor how end users perceive your applications. Ultimately, this is all that matters. Monitoring the infrastructure is not enough.

13

Social media is a great way to monitor your reputation; if your IT is broken, people will talk about it online (blogs, Twitter, etc.).

14

For ITIL[1] v3 Continual Service Improvement, leverage the data gathered by your IT monitoring tools to improve your business services!

---

1. ITIL = Information Technology Infrastructure Library, a collection of best practices for IT practitioners. http://www.itil-officialsite.com/

15

User perception defines the performance of the IT group; reduce negative perceptions through proactive incident management.

16

In many companies, IT Operations is no longer a commodity. CXOs see IT as a strategic business investment.

Section II
People

People are the core of any IT monitoring solution. Without a capable and motivated team in place, you will inevitably fail at keeping your infrastructure running and your business customers satisfied. Automating routine tasks keeps people engaged and focused on value-added activities.

17

Focus your ops team on the important, not just the urgent.

18

Hire the best people, train them well, equip them with the best tools. They are the first line for incident detection and resolution.

19

The head of Infrastructure and Operations now plays a key, strategic role in the business. This is no longer a cost center.

20

ITIL Process Owners define key performance indicators (KPIs). They must bring in requirements from an IT monitoring perspective.

21

Centralize monitoring. Reduce duplication of effort. You don't need multiple teams watching consoles with flashing lights.

22

How many teams do you have managing first-level events? Any number greater than one is too many!

23

Experts love the instant gratification of fixing an issue, but it's not their primary focus. Let the Operations Bridge do its job!

24

If you know the root cause of an incident, only one group needs to respond. This should be your goal if you are serious about reducing cost.

25

Unload day-to-day event management from your subject matter experts. They should focus on their primary jobs, not "firefighting."

26

What % of incidents turn into costly, disruptive escalations to your subject matter experts? Reducing this % generates cost savings.

27

Build a strong team. Do not allow your IT monitoring to become too dependent on one person. This is high risk if they leave.

28

Use an ITIL RACI matrix (responsible, accountable, consulted, informed) to define each role during event, incident, problem mgmt processes.

29

Cross-train and rotate team leaders into new domains or projects. This keeps them fresh, brings new ideas, and generates cross-pollination.

30

PARTICIPATE in (don't just join) an online or in-person community to share best practices with peers.

31

Experts are hard to find. Redirect manpower released from daily operational activities to strategic business projects.

32

ITIL Service Assets =

Resources (tangibles)

+

Capabilities (intangibles).

People's knowledge and

expertise are vital assets.

33

Align the goals of all
your Operations team.
Focus on what matters:
service availability,
mean time to repair, cost
of management.

Section III
Process

Given the complexity of modern IT infrastructures, organizations need robust processes to maintain service levels at agreed-upon levels. While some larger companies may embrace the richness of ITIL v3, others can get by with documenting their own best practices and following them consistently.

34

Consistency counts. A poorly performing infrastructure can be worse than one that is completely broken.

35

Monitor IT holistically—include network, storage, servers, applications, and end-user experience.

36

You must build in and fund monitoring with new applications. Adding it on will not work. This is a key part of the development process.

37

Automate everywhere. Start small, build confidence, and expand—monitor, collect, correlate, determine impact, analyze, and resolve.

38

The Operations Bridge should see ALL alerts and take first actions. Do not allow fragmented alerting paths to emerge.

39

The end goal is to focus as much of the day-to-day operations activity into the lower cost levels of the IT organization.

40

Coordinate your Operations Bridge and Service Desk. Good collaboration will result in high customer satisfaction.

41

Track everything. # of incidents, # of escalations, time to repair, # of people required to fix, service availability, unscheduled downtime.

42

Reuse your existing IT processes when possible, but make incremental changes as needed to drive efficiencies or adapt to new technologies.

43

Build agility into your processes with automatic responses to configuration changes and automated root cause analysis.

44

An average event costs $75 to manually process. Reducing this through automation, for example, generates measureable cost savings.[2]

---

2. A 2009 survey of two VIVIT user group meetings (n=100) found that it costs an average U.S. company $75 to manually process an event. We have further validated this number with several enterprise IT organizations. VIVIT is an independent HP user community. http://www.vivit-worldwide.org/

45

Document your best practices for troubleshooting. Then automate them so everyone consistently performs as well as your best operators.

46

Correlating events requires rules. Either you build them, someone writes them for you, or you create them automatically.

47

Keep the Service Desk informed about incident status with automatic updates. They can assure customers that issues are being resolved.

48

Integrate tools and technologies such that relevant data is passed to the next incident owner during hand-off or escalation processes.

49

Use postmortem analysis to learn and understand the underlying causes of outages or IT problems, not to blame a person or team.

50

Development and operations must work together to build monitoring processes into the software creation process. Some call this "DevOps."

51

End-user monitoring is important, but the initial consumer of alerts must be the Operations Bridge and NOT the application teams.

52

Address IT management during ITIL v3 Service Strategy phase to prevent unexpected costs during Service Design or Service Transition phases.

53

For Agile environments, monitoring the IT infrastructure must be part of the dev/test/QA/release process.

54

Automation is the key to consistency, lower costs, and higher service levels. ALWAYS look to automate IT processes.

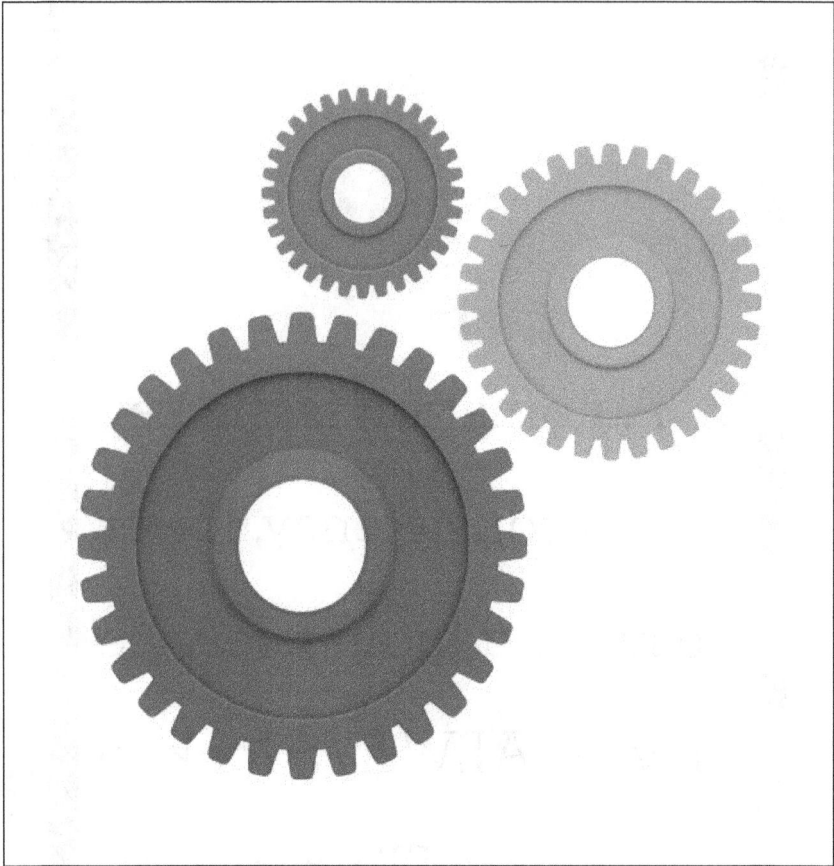

Section IV
Technology

Leading-edge technology, especially automation, can significantly reduce the cost of managing IT infrastructure. Embedding automated operations at each stage of the management process ensures consistent response to recurring problems and generally speeds the time to repair.

55

Complexity = Cost

56

The Operations Bridge needs an up-to-date view of the managed environment so their tools can provide good guidance on what to do next.

57

Use visualization tools to view complex business services. This greatly helps troubleshooting.

58

Empower your Operations Bridge with tools and run-book automation so they can fix as much as possible. Let them DO, not just SEE.

59

Tailor discovery of the
Operations Bridge
view of the IT world to
their needs—enough
detail, rapidly updated
when changes occur.

60

Relating the monitoring information to business services requires an automatically updated model with focused discovery to maintain it.

61

Use classes to organize monitoring by similar types of servers. For example, all database servers can use the same monitoring definitions.

62

Good models drive efficient event correlation. But make sure you automate this process to keep up with changes in your environment.

63

Automate the interface between your event console and ticketing system. When monitoring notifies you of an incident, open a ticket.

64

Bad data is worse than no data. Make sure your monitoring is delivering accurate results. If something feels wrong, check it.

65

Use a configuration management database (CMDB) to strategically track relationships among configuration items.

66

In your CMDB, assign an owner to each configuration item. When a problem arises, you know whom to contact.

67

Automate whatever you can, but only after your processes are working smoothly.

68

Simulate user sessions
to give early warning on
infrastructure problems.
A person will not see a
10% performance drop.
Automated tools will.

69

Look for tools that deliver high value with low maintenance overhead. Otherwise, they will not scale to your environment.

70

It is impossible to anticipate every situation in your IT environment. Use intelligent automation to create and maintain correlation rules.

71

Modern monitoring should include a mobile component so your experts can resolve problems on the go, reducing MTTR.[3]

---

3. MTTR = mean time to repair

72

"Free" is not free unless your time is worth nothing. Think carefully about the total cost of ownership for freeware or open source.

73

Avoid monitoring silos for "special" technologies. Soon the technology will be mainstream and it must be monitored as part of the whole.

74

Chasing symptom events is expensive; use technology to suppress them or correlate them so they are related to the underlying cause event.

75

If you are not in the business of building IT management software, then don't. Buy off-the-shelf tools with pre-integrated components.

Section V
Architecture

Choosing what, where, and how you monitor your IT infrastructure will determine how well you can meet service-level commitments. Good monitoring architecture can make or break the success of your IT management solution.

76

Good IT monitoring delivers the right INFORMATION to the right PEOPLE in the right CONTEXT.

77

Rely on a common data model for collecting system and service-level metrics. This eliminates disagreements over whose data is correct.

78

Filter events at the point of collection to minimize traffic to the Operations Bridge. Correlate everywhere that you can.

79

Use agentless monitoring whenever possible to speed time to deployment. Use agents to get granular data, especially on system performance.

80

If you use multiple databases, federate them to ensure a "single version of the truth."

81

When considering monitoring options, treat virtual servers the same as physical servers unless there is a compelling reason not to do so.

82

Ensure that your monitoring has the reporting capabilities you need. It should provide information for all the roles that will use it.

83

Some companies send correlated events directly to their Service Desk.

84

Standardize wherever possible. This applies to platforms, configurations, databases, as well as monitoring systems.

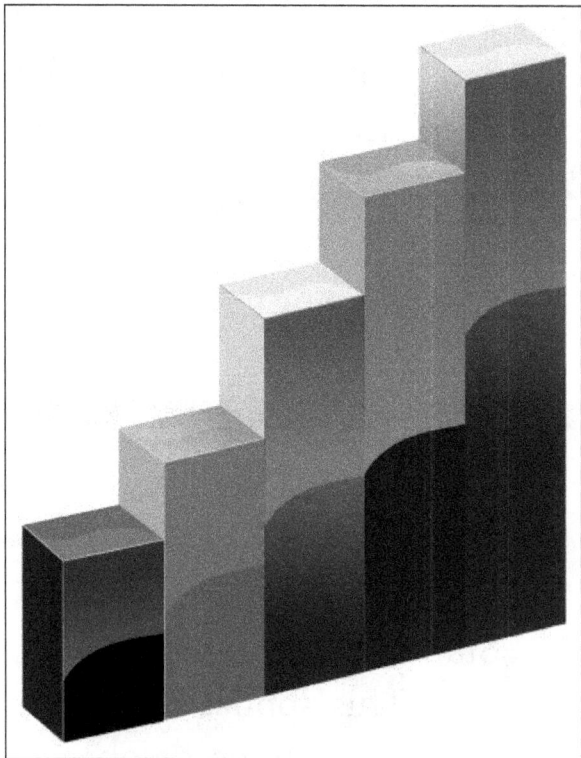

Section VI
Performance Management

Performance management extends beyond just monitoring. It includes disciplines such as reporting and capacity planning. The data sources for performance are the same as for monitoring, but the tools are different, as are the people that use them.

85

The network always used to get blamed for performance problems—now virtualization gets blamed.

86

Performance management is a multi-tiered discipline. Retain data & tools to support each layer: alerting, reporting, diagnostics, planning.

87

Performance management must be business-service-centric, include physical and virtual environments, and deal with dynamic provisioning.

88

In dynamic environments (like vMotion), dynamic threshold-based monitoring (baselining) & dynamic correlation minimizes maintenance effort.

89

If you store performance data on a virtual guest, make sure you have an archive to access this information if the virtual guest disappears.

90

Consolidate cross-domain performance data and response time measures with appropriate granularity to support long-term reporting & planning.

91

Retain diagnostic performance data, at the collection point where possible, for a reasonable duration to support triage.

92

Use historical performance information as the foundation for capacity planning. You will be able to achieve better utilization.

93

The solution to performance problems is not always more hardware. Understand the cause before you jump to conclusions.

94

Detect application availability and performance issues proactively. Fix them before your customer's experience degrades.

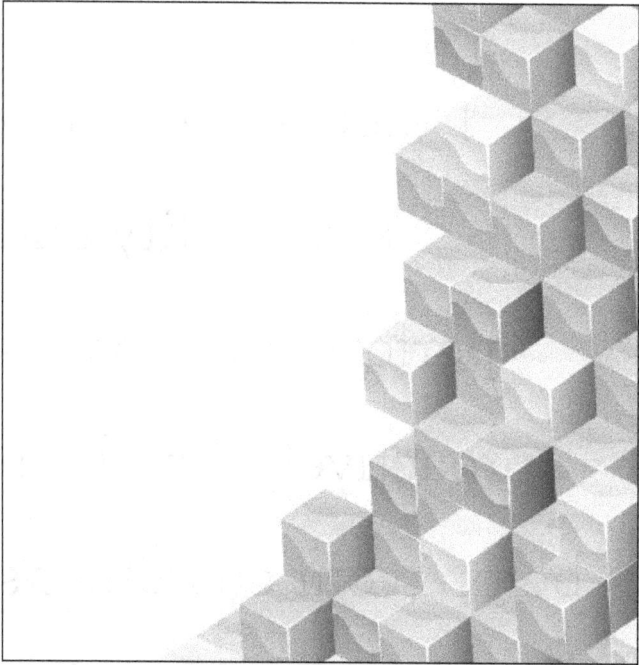

Section VII
Virtualization

Virtualization is one of the biggest technology disruptions in the past decade. It allows organizations to dramatically increase the utilization of their servers. But this can come at a great price if inefficient management practices erode the savings on hardware.

95

Virtualization changes everything. Adjust your core monitoring processes accordingly.

96

Virtualization is dynamic & increases the need for accurate, timely discovery so that monitoring activities can keep up with the real world.

97

Virtual servers can cause multiple virtual guests to fail; they must be monitored as a business critical resource.

98

Virtual guests are just servers with shared hardware. They can still disrupt a business service, so treat them like any other server.

99

Monitoring how virtual guests use server resources is important, but you still need to monitor "inside" the guests to see why issues occur.

100

Manage physical and virtual servers using the same tools and processes.

101

Correlating events across the virtual/physical boundary is difficult. Use an integrated solution to speed troubleshooting and cut MTTR.

102

Follow the VMs.[4] As virtual machines move to a new server, make sure the monitoring goes with it. Automatically.

4. VM = virtual machine

103

Virtualization helps most companies, not all. If you have a compelling reason to use physical servers only, do it.

104

Optimize workload placement on virtual machines using both historical usage patterns and planned demand.

105

Oversizing resources for a VM can degrade VM server performance. (Management overhead for larger VMs is higher.)

106

If you use averages to size and place your VMs, you will end up under-provisioning; if you use peaks, you will end up over-provisioning.

107

Choose the best hypervisor for your needs. It may be more than one. Monitor all using a single, central console to speed troubleshooting.

108

Add value in virtualized environments by discovering underutilized systems. Shut them down and reclaim the capacity.

109

Virtual servers are the new mainframes. Additional disciplines such as capacity planning need to be employed to manage risk.

110

Changes are inevitable. You need a way to keep your service maps current. With virtualization, automation is the only way.

111

Virtual server monitoring has to be integrated into the overall monitoring solution to understand business service impact.

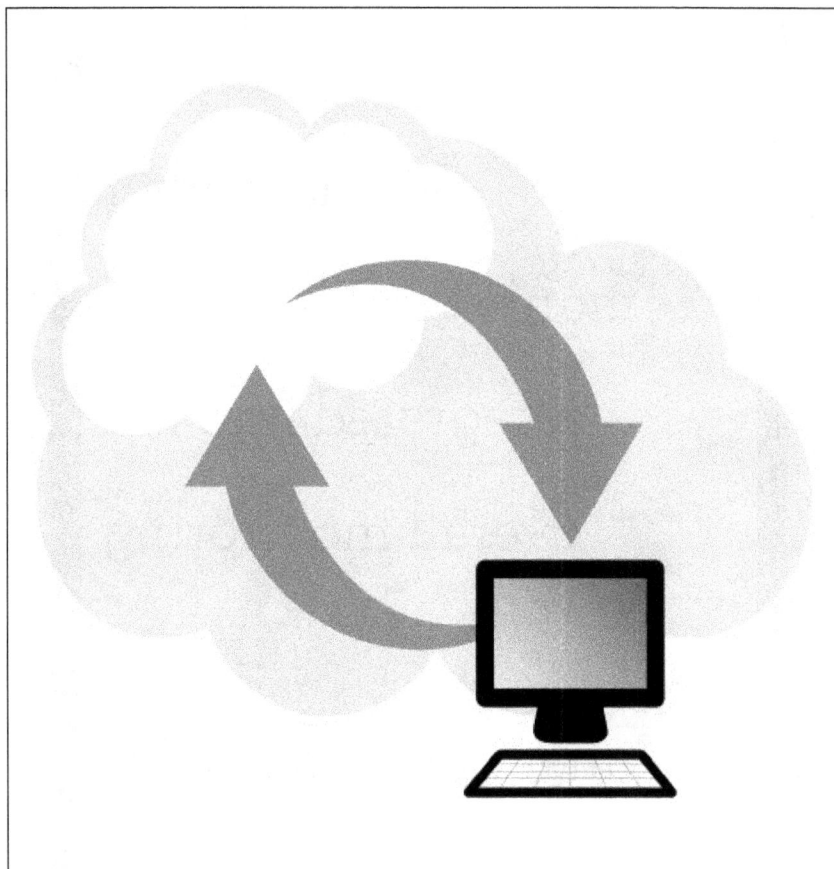

Section VIII
Cloud Computing

Many see cloud computing as the panacea for delivering and managing business services. But how do you monitor the availability and performance provided by your cloud vendor? And, if you are creating a private cloud offering, how do you manage the infrastructure?

112

Cloud computing
is changing the
way in which IT
is built, delivered,
and consumed.

113

The application doesn't know it's running in the cloud. Monitor its availability and performance as you would in an on-premise environment.

114

Monitor cloud services based on how your users perceive them.

115

It does not need to be a major leap to build a private cloud environment; you can make incremental steps starting with what you have now.

116

If you are considering private cloud in the future, build in usage metering and billing today.

117

Data center sprawl? You can scale using someone else's capacity with public cloud.

118

Do worry about what is happening inside the black box (public cloud). Insist on some measurements.

119

Public cloud ≠ Virtualization. Google is the best known example. Private clouds are usually highly virtualized.

120

Companies that offer cloud computing are basically "service providers." Make sure they provide you with the service you are paying for.

121

Trust, but verify. Monitor service levels to ensure you are getting what you paid your cloud provider to deliver.

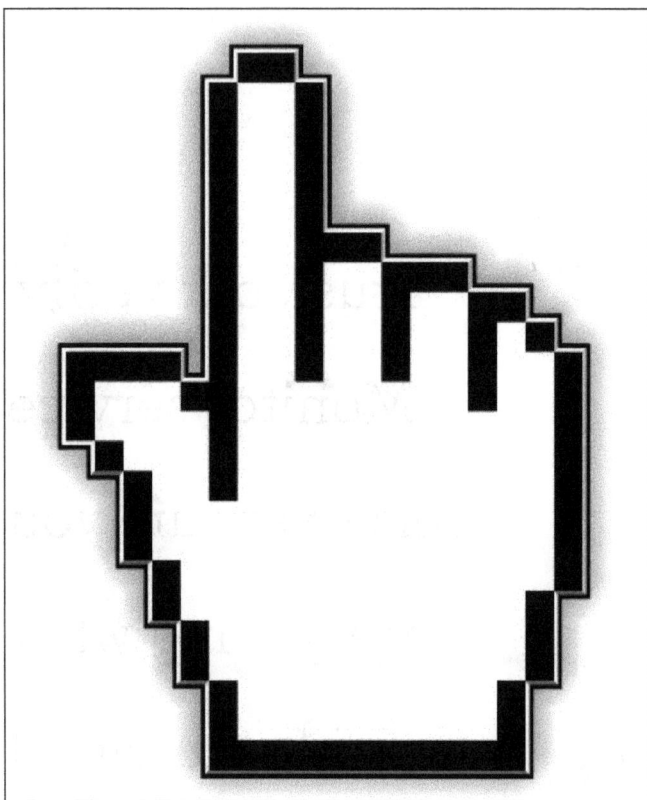

Section IX
Getting Started

If you are reading this book, you are on the right path to improving your IT Operations. Choose one or two ideas from this book that seem achievable, and get them done. Track the return on your investments. Rinse and repeat.

122

Event and performance management only has value if it leads to action.

123

Continuing with your status quo monitoring will likely fail because of the significant structural changes happening in the IT industry.

124

Manage infrastructure holistically. Combine fault, performance, configuration, and IT process automation.

125

Integrate security alerts into your operations management console. Is the CPU spike increased by user demand or a hacker?

126

To start building an Operations Bridge, consolidate all alerts/events into one place to provide complete visibility of the IT environment.

127

Once all events are coming into one place, then deploy technologies to help refine the event stream to highlight causal (actionable) events.

128

Don't allow political agendas or technical objections to undermine an Ops Bridge deployment. Other companies have done it successfully.

129

Integration is very resource intensive, especially as products evolve. Make your vendors do this for you. Keep them honest.

130

What is the true cost of "free" monitoring tools? Consider the labor cost of configuring & maintaining them. 3-year time horizon is typical.

131

Rip & replace is costly & disruptive. Add a new monitoring solution as an overlay or "manager of managers" until ready to retire servers.

132

During ITIL v3 Service Strategy phase, consider IT monitoring processes & tool selection from both financial and demand management aspects.

133

Monitoring must be included in the cost calculations of developing new applications. Add this into your project budget.

134

Operations Bridge staff must help create the IT monitoring solution—don't build in isolation and throw it over the wall.

135

Consider hosted monitoring (SaaS)[5] as a way to get the functionality you need without installing any software or buying any hardware.

5. SaaS = Software as a Service

136

If you can't measure it, you can't manage it. Establish key performance indicators and use the data to drive continuous improvement.

137

Embrace proven best practices to reduce risk.

138

If you want to know what to monitor, check your system log files. Set thresholds to alert you of issues before they become incidents.

139

Have a clear vision of your goal, but implement in manageable, measurable, incremental steps.

140

Consolidation is a process. Aim for a single central console and enjoy the incremental cost savings as you reduce duplication of effort.

About the Authors

Peter Spielvogel leads the global Product Marketing team for the HP Operations Center (formerly OpenView Operations) product portfolio. Since starting his career twenty-five years ago developing software for financial services companies, he has held marketing, sales, and product management positions at Fortune 500 companies and several startups. Peter is ITIL v3 Foundation certified. He speaks internationally on IT Operations topics, including virtualization, automation, cloud computing, and consolidated operations. His education includes an MBA from the Tuck School of Business at Dartmouth and a BS in Engineering from Princeton University. He is based in Silicon Valley, California.

Read his blog at www.hp.com/go/ITOpsBlog

Follow him on Twitter *@HPITOps*

Email Peter at ITOpsBook@gmail.com

Jon Haworth leads Product Marketing for the Service and Operations Bridge within the HP Operations Center product portfolio. He has twenty-five years of experience working for HP across a variety of roles including consulting, pre-sales, and marketing. Jon has designed and implemented large-scale infrastructure management solutions for a number of Fortune 1000 enterprises. Jon is an early adopter and continued advocate for ITIL having gained his ITIL v2 Service Manager certification in 1996. He speaks extensively throughout Europe and Asia on the advantages of consolidating IT management. Jon has a BS degree in Computer Science from Manchester University. He is based outside London in the UK.

Read his blog at www.hp.com/go/ITOpsBlog

Email Jon at ITOpsBook@gmail.com

Sonja Hickey leads Product Marketing for the instrumentation product lines within the HP Operations Center product portfolio. She has twenty years of product marketing, product management, engineering, and consulting experience with privately-held, startup, and Fortune 500 companies. Sonja is ITIL v3 Foundation certified. She speaks frequently throughout the U.S. about IT management best practices. Sonja's education includes an MBA from the University of Chicago GSB and BS and MS degrees in Engineering from the University of Illinois at Urbana-Champaign. She is based near Chicago, Illinois.

Read her blog at www.hp.com/go/ITOpsBlog

Follow her on Twitter *@HPITOps*

Email Sonja at ITOpsBook@gmail.com

The authors are donating all their royalties to the HP Foundation, which funds global disaster relief efforts. The publisher is matching their contribution dollar for dollar.

Other Books in the THiNKaha Series

The THiNKaha book series is for thinking adults who lack the time or desire to read long books, but want to improve themselves with knowledge of the most up-to-date subjects. THiNKaha is a leader in timely, cutting-edge books and mobile applications from relevant experts that provide valuable information in a fun, Twitter-brief format for a fast-paced world.

They are available online at http://thinkaha.com or at other online and physical bookstores.

1. *#BOOK TITLE tweet Book01:* 140 Bite-Sized Ideas for Compelling Article, Book, and Event Titles by Roger C. Parker

2. *#COACHING tweet Book01:* 140 Bite-Sized Insights On Making A Difference Through Executive Coaching by Sterling Lanier

3. *#CONTENT MARKETING tweet Book01:* 140 Bite-Sized Ideas to Create and Market Compelling Content by Ambal Balakrishnan

4. *#CORPORATE CULTURE tweet Book01:* 140 Bite-Sized Ideas to Help You Create a High Performing, Values Aligned Workplace that Employees LOVE by S. Chris Edmonds

5. *#CROWDSOURCING tweet Book01:* 140 Bite-Sized Ideas to Tap into the Wisdom of the Crowd by Kiruba Shankar and Mitchell Levy

6. *#DEATHtweet Book01:* A Well-Lived Life through 140 Perspectives on Death and Its Teachings by Timothy Tosta

7. *#DEATH tweet Book02:* 140 Perspectives on Being a Supportive Witness to the End of Life by Timothy Tosta

8. *#DIVERSITYtweet Book01:* Embracing the Growing Diversity in Our World by Deepika Bajaj

9. *#DREAMtweet Book01:* Inspirational Nuggets of Wisdom from a Rock and Roll Guru to Help You Live Your Dreams by Joe Heuer

10. *#ENTRY LEVEL tweet Book02:* Inspiration for New Professionals by Christine Ruff and Lori Ruff

11. *#ENTRYLEVELtweet Book01:* Taking Your Career from Classroom to Cubicle by Heather R. Huhman

12. *#IT OPERATIONS MANAGEMENT tweet Book01:* Managing Your IT Infrastructure in The Age of Complexity by Peter Spielvogel, Jon Haworth, Sonja Hickey

13. *#JOBSEARCHtweet Book01:* 140 Job Search Nuggets for Managing Your Career and Landing Your Dream Job by Barbara Safani